Step 1
Go to www.openlightbox.com

Step 2
Enter this unique code
ZRVQX58DM

Step 3
Explore your interactive eBook!

Meet My Pet

AV2

DOG

Start!

Share

AV2 is optimized for use on any device

Your interactive eBook comes with...

  Audio Listen to the entire book read aloud

 Videos Watch informative video clips

 Weblinks Gain additional information for research

 Try This! Complete activities and hands-on experiments

 Key Words Study vocabulary, and complete a matching word activity

 Quizzes Test your knowledge

 Slideshows View images and captions

 Share Share titles within your Learning Management System (LMS) or Library Circulation System

 Citation Create bibliographical references following APA, CMOS, and MLA styles

This title is part of our AV2 digital subscription

1-Year K–5 Subscription
ISBN 978-1-7911-3320-7

Access hundreds of AV2 titles with our digital subscription.
Sign up for a FREE trial at **www.openlightbox.com/trial**

The digital components of this book are guaranteed to stay active for at least five years from the date of publication.

DOG

Meet My Pet

CONTENTS

- 4 Adopting a Dog
- 6 Different Dogs
- 8 Dog Care
- 10 Play Time
- 12 Sleeping
- 14 Dog Sounds
- 16 Dog Food
- 18 Dog Needs
- 20 My Pet Dog
- 22 Dog Facts
- 24 Key Words

I want a pet dog.
I need to learn how to take care of her.

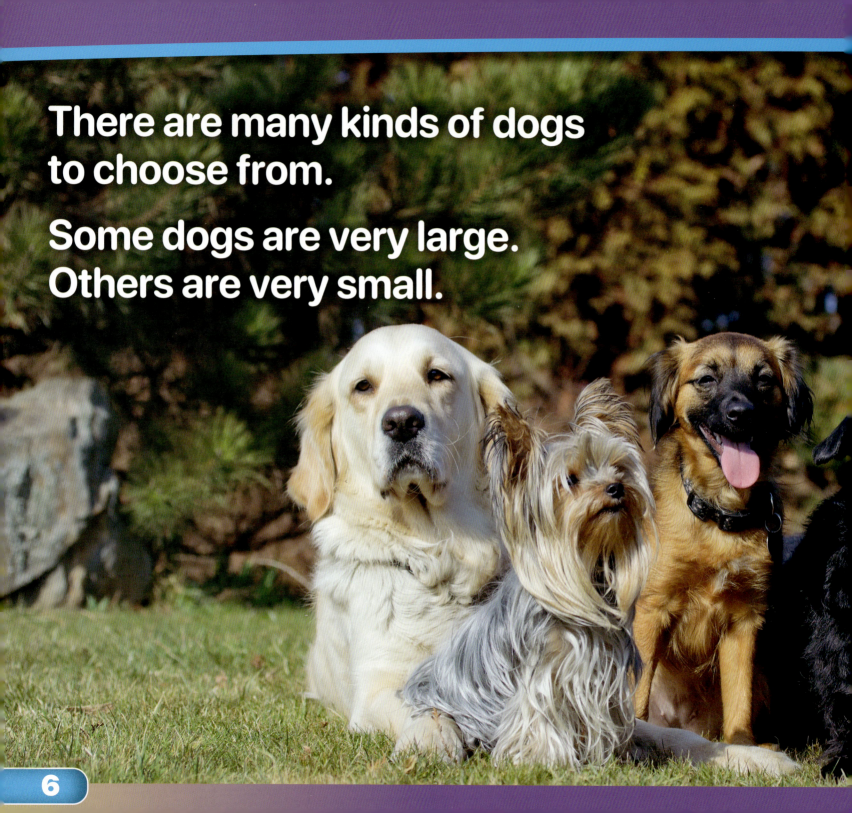

There are many kinds of dogs to choose from.

Some dogs are very large. Others are very small.

Yorkshire Terrier
Less than 7 pounds (3 kilograms)

Pug
Up to 18 pounds (8 kg)

Great Dane
Up to 175 pounds (79 kg)

Golden Retriever
Up to 75 pounds (34 kg)

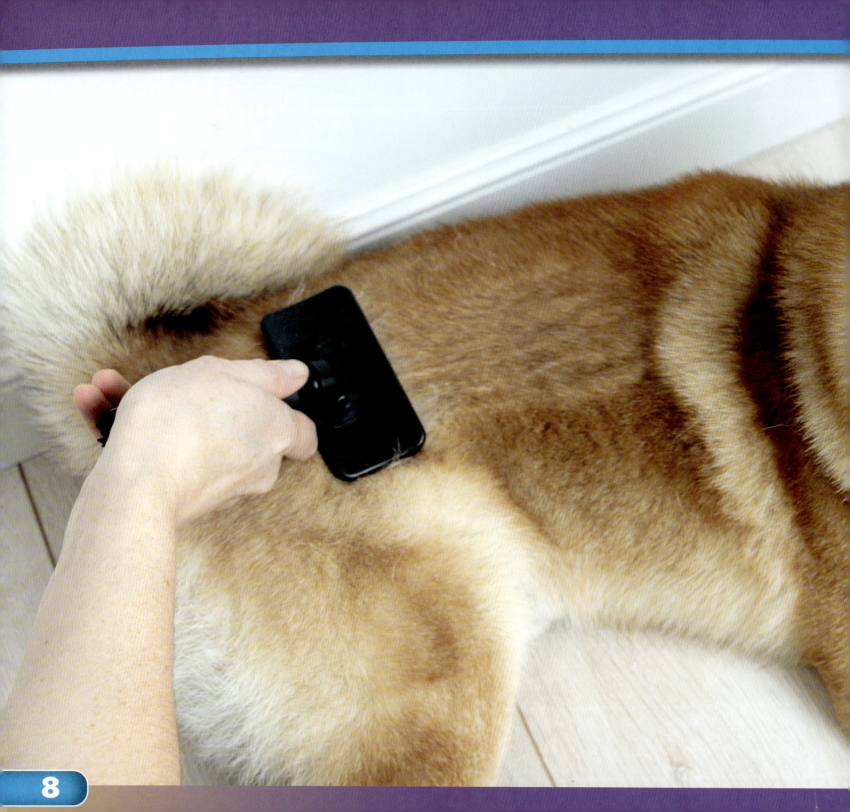

Dogs need help to keep their fur clean.

I will brush my dog often to clean her fur.

My pet dog will need to exercise every day.

I will play fetch with her in our backyard.

DAILY EXERCISE

Labrador Up to **120** minutes of exercise

Jack Russell Up to **90** minutes of exercise

Miniature Pinscher Up to **60** minutes of exercise

French Bulldog Up to **30** minutes of exercise

It is important my dog has a warm place to rest.

I try to stay quiet so she can sleep.

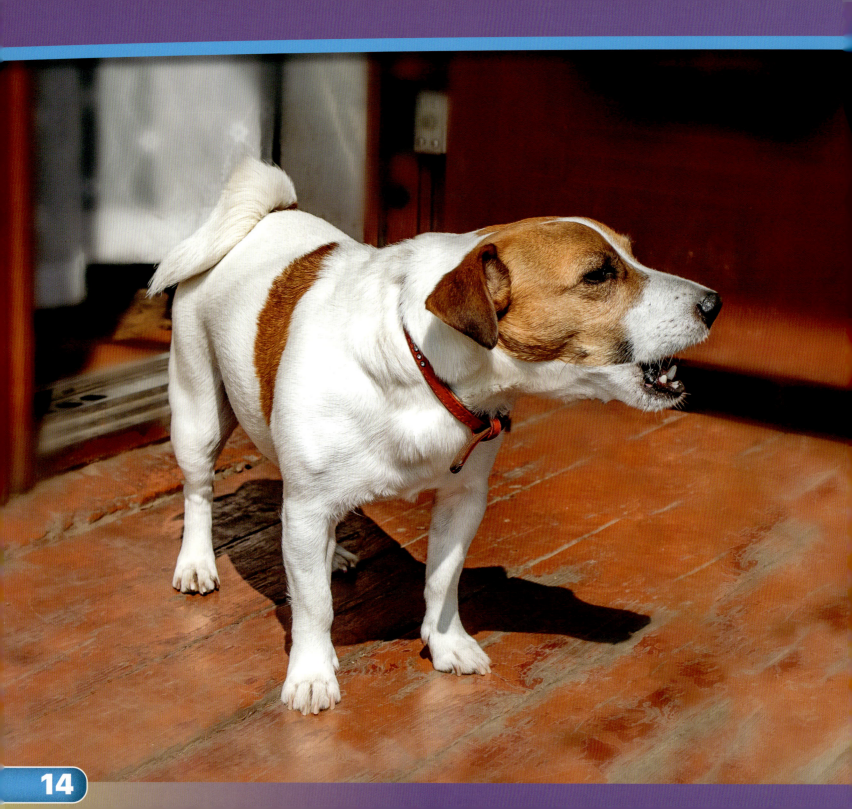

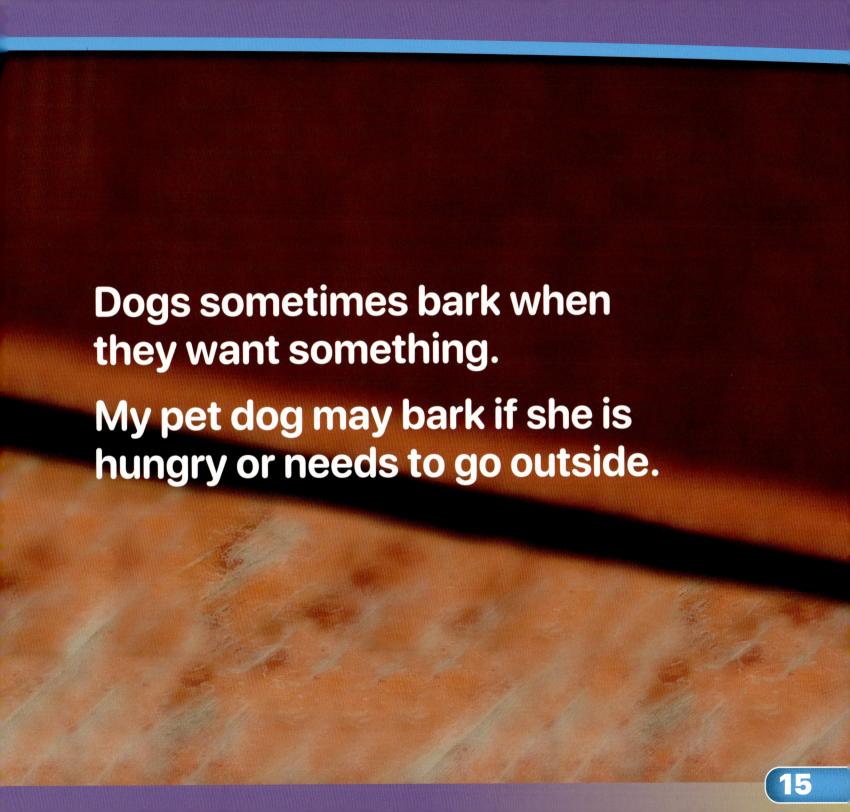

Dogs sometimes bark when they want something.

My pet dog may bark if she is hungry or needs to go outside.

I will feed my pet dog twice a day.

She needs fresh water to drink all day long.

Dogs need to chew on things to keep their teeth healthy.

I will make sure my dog has toys that are safe to chew.

Growing Up

Newborn Puppy
Up to 3 pounds (1.4 kg)
She drinks her mother's milk.
She cannot open her eyes.

1-Month-Old Puppy
Up to 5 pounds (2.7 kg)
She can hear and see.
Her teeth start to grow.

2-Month-Old Puppy
Up to 11 pounds (5 kg)
She learns to play.
She eats solid food.

1-Year-Old Dog
Up to 60 pounds (27 kg)
She learns manners.
She stops growing.

I am ready to take home my pet dog.

I will take great care of her.

THINK ABOUT IT!

What other steps can you take to keep your dog happy and healthy?

DOG FACTS

These pages provide detailed information that expands on the interesting facts found in the book. They are intended to be used by adults as a learning support to help young readers round out their knowledge of each amazing animal featured in the *Meet My Pet* series.

Pages 4–5

I want a pet dog. Humans have kept dogs as pets for thousands of years. It is believed that dogs were the first animals that learned to live with people as pets and service animals. Some dog breeds can be trained to act as guides for people who are visually impaired. Today, one out of every three households in the United States owns a dog.

Pages 6–7

There are many kinds of dogs to choose from. There are about 400 different breeds of dogs. They range in weight from 3 to 175 pounds (1 to 79 kg). A mastiff weighing 343 pounds (156 kg) holds the world record for heaviest dog. The shortest dog on record is a Chihuahua that stood 4 inches (10 cm) tall. Labradors are the most popular dog breed in the world.

Pages 8–9

Dogs need help to keep their fur clean. Dogs should be brushed every few days to reduce shedding and remove dirt. Brushing also promotes healthy skin. Some dog breeds shed more than others and may need to be brushed more frequently. Dogs also need to have their nails trimmed and their eyes, ears, and teeth cleaned. Most dogs only need to be bathed a few times each year.

Pages 10–11

My pet dog will need to exercise every day. Regular exercise provides a good outlet for natural dog behaviors, such as digging, chewing, chasing, and retrieving. Most dogs should be allowed to run for 20 to 30 minutes each day. Individual exercise needs vary, depending on the breed, age, and general health of the dog. Dog owners should use a leash, as well as a harness or collar, when walking their dogs. Leashes help keep dogs safe from cars and other outdoor dangers.

Pages 12–13

It is important my dog has a warm place to rest. Dog beds provide comfort and help keep dogs from sleeping on furniture. Experts recommend that dog owners keep their pet inside the house, except for when it is let out to exercise. If a dog is left outside for more than a short time, it needs access to fresh water and shade on hot days and warm shelter on cold days.

Pages 14–15

Dogs sometimes bark when they want something. Dogs communicate with body movements, facial expressions, and vocal sounds, such as barking. A dog often barks to get its owner's attention when it needs something. Dogs also bark when they are alarmed or feeling playful. The basenji is the only dog breed that cannot bark. Humans can easily misread dog communication. For example, yawning shows a dog is puzzled, not sleepy.

Pages 16–17

I will feed my pet dog twice a day. Puppies up to one year old need two to four meals each day. After a dog's first birthday, one or two meals a day is often sufficient. Veterinarians can help dog owners learn the right amount of food to feed their dogs. Foods such as chocolate, grapes, and raisins are harmful to dogs and should never be offered as treats.

Pages 18–19

Dogs need to chew on things to keep their teeth healthy. Dogs are very playful animals that like to chew. Chewing can help to keep a dog's teeth clean. Large, hard, rubber toys are safe for a dog to chew on and carry around. Small objects, such as string, rubber bands, and small toys, pose a choking hazard, and should not be given to dogs.

Pages 20–21

I am ready to take home my pet dog. People may choose to bring home a dog from a pet store, or they may adopt a dog from an animal shelter. About 20 percent of dogs kept as pets in the United States were adopted from animal shelters. Older dogs often require less attention than puppies. Each dog breed has unique qualities and needs. New dog owners should research what type of dog will be best for their family.

KEY WORDS

Research has shown that as much as 65 percent of all written material published in English is made up of 300 words. These 300 words cannot be taught using pictures or learned by sounding them out. They must be recognized by sight. This book contains 79 common sight words to help young readers improve their reading fluency and comprehension. This book also teaches young readers several important content words, such as proper nouns. These words are paired with pictures to aid in learning and improve understanding.

Page	Sight Words First Appearance
4	a, her, how, I, learn, need, of, take, to, want
6	are, from, kinds, large, many, others, small, some, there, very
7	great, than, up
9	help, keep, my, often, their, will
10	day, every, in, our, play, with
13	can, has, important, is, it, place, she, so, try
15	go, if, may, or, something, sometimes, they, when
16	all, long, water
18	make, on, that, things
19	and, eats, eyes, food, grow, hear, mother, old, open, start, see, stops, year
20	am, home
21	about, think, what, you, your

Page	Content Words First Appearance
4	dog
7	breeds, golden retriever, Great Dane, pug, Yorkshire terrier
9	fur
10	backyard
11	exercise, French bulldog, Jack Russell, Labrador, miniature pinscher
15	outside
18	teeth, toys
19	manners, milk, puppy
21	steps

Published by Lightbox Learning Inc.
276 5th Avenue, Suite 704 #917
New York, NY 10001
Website: www.openlightbox.com

Copyright ©2024 Lightbox Learning Inc.
All rights reserved. No part of this publication may be reproduced, stored in a retrieval system, or transmitted in any form or by any means, electronic, mechanical, photocopying, recording, or otherwise, without the prior written permission of the publisher.

Library of Congress Control Number: 2023932921

ISBN 978-1-7911-5582-7 (hardcover)
ISBN 978-1-7911-5583-4 (softcover)
ISBN 978-1-7911-5584-1 (multi-user eBook)

Printed in Guangzhou, China
1 2 3 4 5 6 7 8 9 0 27 26 25 24 23

062023
100922

Project Coordinator: Sara Cucini   Art Director: Terry Paulhus

Every reasonable effort has been made to trace ownership and to obtain permission to reprint copyright material. The publisher would be pleased to have any errors or omissions brought to its attention so that they may be corrected in subsequent printings.

The publisher acknowledges Getty Images, Alamy, and Shutterstock as the primary image suppliers for this title.